REAL ESTATE

INVESTMENT

Step by step guide to Unlocking Success and Navigating the Pitfalls of Real Estate Investment and Proven Strategies for Growth

By: James N. Wagner

Copyright © 2024
[James N. Wagner].

All rights reserved. No part of this ebook, "Real Estate Investment," may be reproduced, distributed, or transmitted in any form or by any means, including photocopying, recording, or other electronic or mechanical methods, without the prior written permission of the publisher, except in the case of brief quotations embodied in critical reviews and certain other noncommercial uses permitted by copyright law. For permission requests, write to the publisher, addressed "Attention: Permissions Coordinator," at the address provided within this ebook.

Table of contents

Introduction.. 8
    Significance of Steering Clear of Errors.......... 10
    Effect on Finances and Investments............... 11
CHAPTER 1:WHAT IS REAL ESTATE INVESTMENT.. 14
Chapter 2: Common Errors in the Selection of Properties.. 18
    Neglecting future development plans..............21
    Ignoring neighborhood and location research.24
    Ignoring property inspection and evaluation... 27
Chapter 3.Investment and Financing Mistakes 30
    Poor Budgeting and Financial Planning.......... 33
Chapter 4:Pathways in Law and Documentation. 38
    Ignoring legal counsel and doing due diligence.. 41
    Inaccurate or lacking documentation and breaking zoning laws and regulations............. 44
Chapter 5. Ignoring Rental Market Dynamics.. 50
    Failing to Conduct Market Analysis..................52
    Neglecting Market Trends and Analysis..........55
    Excessive Reduction in Property Value.......... 56
Chapter 6:Oversights of Management and Maintenance.. 60
    The Costly Errors of Inadequate Property Management Techniques............................... 62

Ignored Maintenance and Repair Problems... 65

Inability to Plan for Emergencies.....................68

Chapter 7:Mistakes in Deal-Making and Negotiation... 71

Poor Ability to Negotiate..................................74

Chapter 8:Mistakes in the Management and Selection of Tenants.. 79

Chapter 9:Mistakes in Tax and Regulatory Compliance..83

Lack of understanding of the benefits and implications of taxes..86

Failure to follow local regulations....................88

Chapter 10:Lack of Risk Management and Diversification.. 91

Concentration of Risk in One Asset or Location. 93

Lack of Risk Mitigation Techniques.................96

Chapter 11:Professional and Ethical Conduct Slips.. 103

Fiduciary duty breaches................................ 106

Conflict of interest concernsb........................ 109

Chapter 12:Results and Suggestions............. 113

The Value of Learning from Mistakes............ 116

Techniques for Steering Clear of Typical Pitfalls. 118

Ongoing Learning and Development in real estate practice...121

Chapter 13: Unlocking success in real estate investment.. 125

Conclusion.. 129

Introduction

In the realm of real estate, fortunes are made and lost, dreams realized and shattered, all amidst the backdrop of brick and mortar. Behind every transaction, every listing, and every purchase lies a story - stories of triumph and tales of woe. Yet, amidst the glitz and glamour, the allure of wealth and success, lurk the shadows of mistakes that have befallen many unsuspecting investors and homeowners.

Consider the tale of the ambitious investor, John. With dreams of financial independence and visions of grandeur, John ventured into the world of real estate with fervor. Armed with confidence and a sizeable bankroll, he dove headfirst into his first investment property, a quaint fixer-upper in an up-and-coming neighborhood.

Excited by the prospect of turning a profit, John neglected to conduct thorough research and due diligence. Blind to the warning signs, he overpaid for the property, failing to recognize the subtle nuances of market valuation. Ignoring the age-old adage "location, location, location," John dismissed the significance of neighborhood dynamics, only to later realize the impact it would have on property appreciation.

As renovations began, John's initial budget proved woefully inadequate, as unforeseen expenses mounted with

each passing day. Caught in a whirlwind of escalating costs, he found himself sinking deeper into debt, a victim of his own miscalculations.

Despite his best intentions, John failed to anticipate shifts in the market, leaving him vulnerable to economic downturns and fluctuating demand. Overleveraged and overstretched, he struggled to weather the storm, his once-promising venture now teetering on the brink of collapse.

In the end, John's story serves as a cautionary tale, a stark reminder of the pitfalls that await the unprepared and the unwary in the world of real estate. From lack of research and overpaying for property to underestimating renovation costs and neglecting market trends, his missteps echo the sentiments of countless others who have fallen prey to the attraction of fast rewards and rapid wealth.

As we embark on this journey through the landscape of real estate, let us heed the lessons of those who have gone before us, learning from their mistakes and forging a path towards success fortified by knowledge, prudence, and foresight.

Significance of Steering Clear of Errors

Avoiding mistakes in real estate is crucial for several reasons:

1. **Financial Stability:** Errors can lead to financial losses, affecting your investment returns, cash flow, and long-term wealth accumulation.
2. **Legal Compliance:** Mistakes may result in legal troubles, fines, or even lawsuits, tarnishing your reputation and disrupting business operations.

3. **Risk Management:** By minimizing errors, you reduce the risk of unforeseen challenges, market fluctuations, and potential downturns in the real estate market.

4. **Reputation Preservation:** Maintaining a reputation for competence and integrity is essential in real estate. Errors can damage your credibility and deter future business opportunities.

5. **Long-Term Success:** Avoiding mistakes fosters sustainable growth and longevity in the real estate industry, enabling you to build a robust portfolio and achieve your financial goals over time.

Effect on Finances and Investments

The impact of mistakes on finances and investments in real estate can be profound:

1. **Financial Losses:** Errors such as overpaying for a property, underestimating renovation costs, or misjudging rental income potential can lead to immediate financial losses.

2. **Reduced Profitability:** Mistakes can decrease the profitability of real estate investments by

diminishing rental yields, increasing expenses, or lowering property values.

3. **Negative Cash Flow:** Poor decisions may result in negative cash flow, where expenses exceed rental income, putting a strain on finances and hindering the ability to cover mortgage payments and other costs.

4. **Impaired Liquidity:** Some mistakes can tie up capital or assets, reducing liquidity and limiting the ability to take advantage of other investment opportunities or address unforeseen financial needs.

5. **Debt Burden:** Overleveraging or taking on excessive debt to finance real estate investments can lead to financial strain, higher interest payments, and increased risk of default or foreclosure.

6. **Opportunity Cost:** Resources spent rectifying mistakes could have been allocated to more profitable ventures, causing missed opportunities for growth and wealth accumulation.

7. **Portfolio Diversification:** Errors can skew the diversification of investment portfolios, exposing investors to higher levels of risk and reducing the effectiveness of risk management strategies.

8. **Long-Term Returns:** Cumulative effects of mistakes may erode long-term investment returns, impacting retirement savings, wealth preservation, and overall financial security.

In essence, the financial repercussions of mistakes in real estate underscore the importance of thorough research, prudent decision-making, and ongoing risk management to safeguard investments and maximize returns.

CHAPTER 1: WHAT IS REAL ESTATE INVESTMENT

Real estate investment is the acquisition, ownership, management, rental, or sale of property for the purpose of generating profit. It encompasses a wide range of assets including residential, commercial, industrial, and agricultural properties, as well as vacant land and development projects. Overview of real estate investment:

1. **Types of Real Estate Investment:**

- **Residential Real Estate:** This includes single-family homes, condominiums, townhouses, and multifamily properties like apartment buildings.

- **Commercial Real Estate:** Commercial properties include office buildings, retail spaces, warehouses, hotels, and mixed-use developments.
- **Industrial Real Estate:** This category includes properties such as factories, manufacturing plants, distribution centers, and industrial parks.
- **Land**: Investing in undeveloped land for future development or as a long-term investment strategy.

- **Real Estate Investment Trusts (REITs):** REITs allow investors to buy shares in a professionally managed portfolio of real estate properties, providing exposure to the real estate market without direct property ownership.

2. **Strategies for Real Estate Investment:**

- **Buy and Hold**: Purchasing properties with the intention of holding onto them for the long term, generating rental income and potentially benefiting from appreciation over time.
- **Fix and Flip**: Buying properties in need of renovation or repair, improving them, and selling them quickly for a profit.
- **Wholesaling**: Acting as an intermediary by finding discounted properties and selling them to other investors for a fee.
- **Real Estate Development**: Investing in the construction or renovation of properties to create value, such as building new residential communities or commercial complexes.

3. **Key Factors Influencing Real Estate Investment:**

• **Market Conditions:** Economic factors, supply and demand dynamics, interest rates, and local market trends impact the profitability of real estate investments.
• **Location**: The desirability and location of a property greatly affect its value and potential for appreciation.
• **Financing**: Access to financing options, such as mortgages, loans, or partnership agreements, can significantly impact investment opportunities.
• **Property Management:** Effective property management is crucial for maximizing rental income, maintaining property value, and minimizing vacancies.

4. **Risks and Considerations:**

• **Market Volatility:** Real estate markets can be subject to fluctuations, impacting property values and investment returns.

• **Liquidity**: Real estate investments can be less liquid compared to other asset classes, as it may take time to sell a property and convert it into cash.

• **Regulatory and Legal Considerations**: Real estate investments are subject to various

regulations, zoning laws, and tax implications that investors need to navigate.
• **Maintenance and Operational Costs:** Property ownership entails expenses such as maintenance, repairs, insurance, and property taxes, which can affect overall profitability.

5. **Benefits of Real Estate Investment**:

• **Potential for Appreciation:** Real estate historically tends to appreciate over time, providing investors with potential capital gains.
• **Income Generation:** Rental properties generate ongoing rental income, offering a steady stream of cash flow.
• **Diversification**: Real estate can serve as a diversification tool within an investment portfolio, reducing overall risk exposure.
• **Tax Advantages**: Real estate investors may benefit from tax deductions, depreciation allowances, and other favorable tax treatments.

REAL ESTATE INVESTMENT offers opportunities for wealth creation, income generation, and portfolio diversification. However, it requires careful research, due diligence, and risk management to maximize returns and mitigate potential risks.

Chapter 2: Common Errors in the Selection of Properties

Selecting the right property is paramount in real estate investment. Here's a comprehensive look at the errors often made in this crucial stage:

1. **Lack of Research on Location and Neighborhood:** Failure to thoroughly research the location and neighborhood can lead to investing in areas with declining property values, high crime rates, or poor amenities.

2. **Ignoring Future Development Plans:** Neglecting to investigate future development plans

in the area can result in investing in properties that may be negatively impacted by upcoming construction or zoning changes.

3. **Overlooking Property Inspection and Evaluation:** Skipping or rushing through property inspections can lead to unforeseen issues such as structural defects, pest infestations, or environmental hazards, which can significantly impact the property's value and investment potential.

4. **Ignoring Property Type Suitability:** Investing in a property type that doesn't align with your investment goals or expertise, such as commercial real estate without prior experience, can lead to challenges in management and lower returns.

5. **Underestimating Renovation Costs:** Failing to accurately assess the cost of necessary renovations or repairs can result in budget overruns, delays in project completion, and reduced profitability.

6. **Overlooking Property Size and Layout:** Not considering factors like property size, layout, and configuration in relation to target tenant demographics or market demand can lead to difficulties in attracting and retaining tenants.

7. **Neglecting Property Appreciation Potential:** Investing in properties with limited potential for appreciation due to factors like market saturation, declining demand, or lack of infrastructure development can result in stagnant or negative returns over time.

8. **Ignoring Environmental Factors:** Disregarding environmental factors such as proximity to industrial sites, flood zones, or natural disaster risks can lead to increased insurance costs, property damage, or difficulty selling the property in the future.

9. **Failing to Consider Property Management Requirements:** Investing in properties that require intensive or specialized property management without adequate resources or expertise can lead to operational challenges, increased costs, and lower returns.

10. **Not Accounting for Legal and Regulatory Constraints:** Overlooking legal and regulatory constraints such as zoning laws, building codes, or homeowners' association regulations can lead to compliance issues, fines, or legal disputes.

11. **Relying Solely on Emotion or Intuition:** Making investment decisions based solely on emotion or intuition without conducting thorough due diligence and financial analysis can lead to biased decision-making and increased risk of poor outcomes.

12. **Failing to Seek Professional Advice:** Not seeking advice from real estate professionals, such as agents, brokers, or legal advisors, can result in overlooking critical factors or making uninformed decisions that negatively impact the investment.

By avoiding these common errors and conducting comprehensive due diligence, investors can improve their chances of selecting properties that align with their investment goals and offer favorable returns over the long term.

Neglecting future development plans

Success in the fast-paced real estate industry frequently depends on meticulous preparation and foresight.. One critical aspect that can make or break a property investment is the consideration of future development plans. Neglecting to account for future development can lead to missed opportunities, decreased property value, and ultimately, financial loss. In this comprehensive content, we'll delve into the ramifications of neglecting future development plans in real estate and offer insights into how to avoid this costly mistake.

1. **Understanding Future Development Plans:** Future development plans encompass a range of factors that can influence the value and potential of a property. This includes zoning regulations,

infrastructure projects, demographic shifts, and urban development initiatives. Ignoring or failing to anticipate these plans can result in significant consequences for property investors.

2. **Impact on Property Value:** Failure to consider future development plans can lead to stagnation or even depreciation in property value. For example, if a new highway or commercial development is slated to be built nearby, properties in the vicinity may experience increased noise pollution or reduced accessibility, thereby lowering their desirability and value.

3. **Missed Opportunities:** Neglecting future development plans can also mean missing out on lucrative opportunities for property enhancement or redevelopment. For instance, failing to recognize a neighborhood's potential for gentrification may result in investors overlooking undervalued properties that could later yield substantial returns.

4. **Regulatory Risks:** Land use policy and zoning laws are crucial to the development of real estate. . Failure to align with these regulations or anticipate changes in zoning laws can lead to regulatory hurdles, delays, and even legal disputes that can impede property development and erode investor confidence.

5. **Strategies to Avoid Neglecting Future Development Plans:**

a. **Conduct Thorough Due Diligence:** Research and analyze local zoning ordinances, municipal plans, and infrastructure projects to identify potential opportunities and risks associated with future development.

b. **Engage with Local Authorities:** Establishing relationships with local government officials and planning departments can provide valuable insights into upcoming development initiatives and regulatory changes that may impact property investments.

c. **Stay Abreast of Market Trends:** Monitor market trends, demographic shifts, and economic indicators to anticipate changes in property demand and identify emerging opportunities for investment and development.

d. **Partner with Experienced Professionals:** Seek guidance from real estate professionals, including developers, urban planners, and legal advisors, who can offer expertise and strategic guidance to navigate complex regulatory landscapes and capitalize on future development opportunities.

Neglecting future development plans in real estate is a critical mistake that can have far-reaching consequences for investors. By understanding the importance of foresight, conducting thorough due diligence, and staying informed about market trends and regulatory changes, investors can mitigate risks and position themselves to capitalize on emerging opportunities for property development and investment success. Remember, in real estate, the key to success lies in planning for the future today.

Ignoring neighborhood and location research

When it comes to buying or investing in real estate, one of the most common and costly mistakes people make is ignoring thorough research into the neighborhood and location. While factors like the condition of the property and its price are important, the neighborhood and location play a significant role in determining the value, desirability, and potential return on investment of a property. Here's why ignoring neighborhood and location research can be detrimental:

1. **Property Value Fluctuations:** The value of a property can be heavily influenced by its location. Desirable neighborhoods with good schools, low crime rates, and proximity to amenities like parks, shopping centers, and public transportation tend to have higher property values and appreciate more over time. Conversely, properties in less desirable

neighborhoods or those experiencing economic decline may see stagnant or declining property values.

2. **Rental Income and Tenant Quality:** For rental properties, the neighborhood and location can impact the rental income you can command and the quality of tenants you attract. Tenants are often willing to pay higher rents for properties located in safe, well-maintained neighborhoods with access to amenities and employment opportunities. Conversely, properties in less desirable neighborhoods may struggle to attract reliable tenants or command competitive rental rates.

3. **Resale Potential:** Whether you're buying a property to live in or as an investment, it's essential to consider its resale potential. Properties located in desirable neighborhoods are typically easier to sell and tend to appreciate more over time, providing a better return on investment when it comes time to sell. Ignoring neighborhood research can result in purchasing a property with limited resale potential, making it challenging to sell or requiring significant time and investment to attract buyers.

4. **Quality of Life:** Beyond financial considerations, the neighborhood and location also impact your quality of life. Factors such as safety, access to amenities, commute times, and the sense of community can significantly influence your overall satisfaction with a property. Ignoring neighborhood research may mean ending up in an area that doesn't align with your lifestyle preferences or

needs, leading to dissatisfaction and regret down the line.

5. **Future Development and Infrastructure Projects:** Researching the neighborhood and location can also provide insights into future development plans and infrastructure projects that may impact property values and quality of life. For example, planned transportation improvements, new schools, or commercial developments can enhance the desirability and value of a neighborhood. Conversely, projects like highway expansions or industrial developments may have negative effects on property values and livability.

ignoring neighborhood and location research in real estate can be a costly mistake with long-term consequences. It's essential to thoroughly investigate the neighborhood, considering factors such as property values, rental income potential, resale value, quality of life, and future development plans before making a purchasing decision. By prioritizing neighborhood research, you can make informed decisions that align with your financial goals and lifestyle preferences, ultimately maximizing the value and satisfaction derived from your real estate investment.

Ignoring property inspection and evaluation

Ignoring property inspection and evaluation in real estate can be a costly mistake that many buyers and sellers make. Whether due to eagerness to close a deal quickly or ignorance of potential issues, neglecting this crucial step can lead to significant financial and emotional repercussions. Here's a comprehensive look at why property inspection and evaluation are essential in real estate transactions:

1. **Identifying Structural Issues:** Property inspections reveal structural defects that may not be visible to the untrained eye. Issues such as foundation cracks, roof damage, plumbing leaks, and electrical problems can be identified during an inspection. Ignoring these issues can result in expensive repairs down the line.

2. **Assessing Safety Concerns:** Inspections also assess the safety of the property. This includes checking for mold, asbestos, radon, and other hazardous materials. Ignoring safety concerns can

put occupants at risk and may lead to legal liabilities.

3. **Estimating Repair Costs:** Property inspections help buyers and sellers understand the true condition of the property and estimate the cost of necessary repairs. Ignoring this step can lead to unexpected expenses and financial strain after the transaction is completed.

4. **Negotiating Power:** Armed with inspection reports, buyers have leverage to negotiate repairs or a lower purchase price. Sellers can address issues upfront or adjust the selling price accordingly. Ignoring inspection results may result in disputes and failed negotiations.

5. **Protecting Investment:** Real estate is a significant investment, and thorough inspections protect buyers from investing in a property with hidden problems. Sellers benefit from inspections by ensuring their property is in the best possible condition for sale. Ignoring inspections jeopardizes the investment for both parties.

6. **Legal Compliance:** In many jurisdictions, property inspections are required by law. Ignoring inspection requirements can lead to legal consequences, including fines, penalties, and potential lawsuits. It's essential to adhere to regulatory standards to avoid legal complications.

7. **Peace of Mind:** A comprehensive property inspection provides peace of mind to both buyers and sellers. Buyers can proceed with confidence knowing the property's condition, while sellers can

demonstrate transparency and integrity in the transaction. Ignoring inspections can lead to anxiety and uncertainty throughout the process.

8. **Long-Term Value:** Addressing issues identified during inspections preserves the long-term value of the property. Ignoring problems may lead to further deterioration and decreased property value over time. Investing in inspections ensures the property maintains its value for future resale or rental opportunities.

ignoring property inspection and evaluation in real estate transactions is a risky decision with potentially severe consequences. Whether you're buying or selling a property, investing in thorough inspections is essential for protecting your investment, ensuring safety and compliance, and facilitating a successful transaction. By prioritizing inspections, you can mitigate risks and make informed decisions that benefit all parties involved.

Chapter 3. Investment and Financing Mistakes

Real estate investment can be highly lucrative, but it's also fraught with potential pitfalls, especially when it comes to financing. From over-leveraging to poor due diligence, here's a comprehensive look at common investment and financing mistakes in real estate:

1. **Over-Leveraging**: Taking on too much debt can be tempting when interest rates are low, but it can also leave investors vulnerable during economic downturns or fluctuations in the real estate market.
   •**Solution**: Practice conservative leverage by maintaining a healthy debt-to-equity ratio and

ensuring that rental income covers mortgage payments comfortably.

2. **Lack of Due Diligence:** Failing to thoroughly research a property, its location, market trends, and potential risks can lead to costly mistakes.

   • **Solution:** Conduct extensive due diligence, including property inspections, market analysis, and evaluating comparable sales, to mitigate risks and make informed investment decisions.

3. **Underestimating Expenses:** Ignoring or underestimating expenses such as maintenance, repairs, property taxes, and insurance can eat into profits and disrupt cash flow.

   • **Solution:** Create a detailed budget that includes all potential expenses and factor them into your financial projections to ensure realistic expectations.

4. **Ignoring Market Trends:** Investing without considering current and future market trends can lead to buying in oversaturated markets, overpaying for properties, or investing in declining areas.

   • **Solution:** Stay informed about local and national real estate trends, demographics, economic indicators, and regulatory changes to make strategic investment decisions.

5. **Poor Financing Choices:** Choosing the wrong financing option, such as adjustable-rate mortgages (ARMs) with unpredictable interest rate fluctuations, can increase risk and volatility.

• **Solution:** Evaluate various financing options, including fixed-rate mortgages, commercial loans, and government-backed loans, to find the most suitable option based on your investment goals and risk tolerance.

6. **Neglecting Cash Reserves:** Failing to maintain adequate cash reserves for unexpected expenses, vacancies, or economic downturns can leave investors vulnerable to financial distress or foreclosure.

   • **Solution:** Set aside a contingency fund to cover unexpected expenses and maintain sufficient liquidity to weather periods of reduced cash flow.

7. **Overestimating Rental Income:** Relying on overly optimistic rental income projections without considering market conditions, vacancies, or potential rental defaults can lead to cash flow shortages.

   • **Solution:** Conduct thorough market research to accurately estimate rental income and vacancy rates, and incorporate conservative projections into your financial analysis.

8. **Lack of Diversification**: Concentrating investments in a single property type, location, or market segment increases exposure to specific risks and limits potential returns.

   • **Solution:** Diversify your real estate portfolio by investing in different property types, geographic areas, and market segments to spread risk and maximize potential returns.

9. **Emotional Decision-Making:** Allowing emotions to drive investment decisions, such as purchasing a property based on personal preferences rather than financial analysis, can lead to costly mistakes.

• **Solution:** Approach real estate investment with a disciplined, rational mindset, relying on data-driven analysis and financial metrics rather than emotional impulses.

10. **Failure to Plan Exit Strategies:** Neglecting to plan for potential exit strategies, such as selling, refinancing, or transitioning to long-term ownership, can limit flexibility and hinder profitability.

• **Solution:** Develop comprehensive exit strategies based on various scenarios, market conditions, and investment objectives to optimize returns and mitigate risks.

avoiding investment and financing mistakes in real estate requires thorough research, prudent decision-making, and disciplined financial management. By addressing these common pitfalls and implementing proactive strategies, investors can enhance their chances of success and build a resilient real estate portfolio.

Poor Budgeting and Financial Planning

Real estate investment can be lucrative, but it also comes with its fair share of risks and challenges. One of the most critical aspects of successful real estate investing is effective budgeting and financial planning. Poor budgeting and financial planning can lead to significant mistakes that can derail even the most promising real estate ventures. In this comprehensive guide, we'll explore the common pitfalls of inadequate budgeting and financial planning in real estate investments and provide strategies to avoid them.

1. **Underestimating Expenses:** One of the most common mistakes in real estate investment is underestimating expenses. This includes not only the purchase price of the property but also ongoing costs such as maintenance, repairs, property taxes, insurance, and utilities.
   • Failure to accurately budget for these expenses can quickly eat into potential profits and lead to financial strain or even failure to sustain the investment.
2. **Overleveraging:** Overleveraging occurs when an investor borrows too much money to finance a

real estate investment, resulting in high levels of debt relative to the property's value.

• Leverage may increase profits in a rising market but it can also increase losses in a falling one. Overleveraging increases financial risk and can lead to foreclosure or bankruptcy if the property fails to generate sufficient income to cover debt payments.

3. **Ignoring Contingencies:** Real estate investments are inherently unpredictable, and unexpected expenses or vacancies can arise at any time.

• Failing to account for contingencies in the budget can leave investors vulnerable to financial setbacks. It's crucial to set aside reserves for unforeseen circumstances to mitigate risk and ensure the sustainability of the investment.

4. **Neglecting Market Analysis:** Inadequate market analysis is another common mistake in real estate investing. Ignoring market trends, demographics, and economic indicators can lead to poor investment decisions.

• Without a thorough understanding of the local market dynamics, investors may overpay for properties, invest in declining neighborhoods, or misjudge rental demand, leading to financial losses.

5. **Overestimating Rental Income:** Overestimating rental income is a frequent error among novice real estate investors. Setting unrealistic rental rates based on optimistic projections can result in vacancies or difficulty attracting tenants.

- It's essential to conduct thorough market research to determine competitive rental rates and factor in potential vacancies when budgeting for rental income.

6. **Lack of Exit Strategy:** A lack of exit strategy is a critical oversight in real estate investing. Without a clear plan for selling or exiting the investment, investors may find themselves unable to liquidate the property when needed.

- Whether it's due to changing market conditions, financial constraints, or personal circumstances, having a well-defined exit strategy is essential for mitigating risk and maximizing returns.

Effective budgeting and financial planning are fundamental to successful real estate investing. Avoiding the common pitfalls of poor budgeting and financial planning requires diligence, market knowledge, and a strategic approach. By accurately assessing expenses, avoiding overleveraging, planning for contingencies, conducting thorough market analysis, realistic income projections, and developing a solid exit strategy, investors can minimize risk and optimize their chances of success in the dynamic world of real estate investing.

Chapter 4: Pathways in Law and Documentation

Real estate transactions involve a complex web of legalities and documentation. Whether you're buying, selling, leasing, or renting property, understanding the pathways in law and documentation is crucial to avoid costly mistakes. Here's a comprehensive guide to navigating this terrain and sidestepping common pitfalls:

1. **Understanding Legal Frameworks:** Local Regulations, Real estate laws vary by jurisdiction. Familiarize yourself with the specific regulations governing property transactions in your area.

- **Zoning Laws:** Be aware of zoning ordinances that dictate how land can be used. Failure to comply can result in issues like fines or inability to develop the property as planned.

2. **Due Diligence:** Title Search, Conduct a thorough title search to uncover any liens, encumbrances, or ownership disputes that could complicate the transaction.

- **Environmental Assessment:** Assess environmental risks associated with the property, such as contamination or ecological restrictions.

• **Survey:** Obtain an accurate survey of the property boundaries to avoid disputes over land rights.
3. **Contracts and Agreements:** Purchase Agreement, Ensure all terms of the sale are clearly outlined in the purchase agreement, including price, contingencies, and timelines.
   • **Lease Agreements:** Draft comprehensive lease agreements that address responsibilities of both landlords and tenants to prevent misunderstandings.
   • **Legal Review:** Have contracts reviewed by legal professionals to identify any ambiguities or clauses that could be detrimental to your interests.
4. **Financing and Documentation: Mortgage Documents:** Understand the terms of your mortgage agreement and review all loan documents carefully before signing.
   • **Insurance Policies:** Obtain appropriate insurance coverage for the property to protect against risks like fire, theft, and liability.
   • **Tax Documentation:** Stay compliant with tax regulations by maintaining accurate records and filing required documentation on time.
5. **Compliance and Permits:** Building Permits,Obtain necessary permits before initiating construction or renovations to avoid legal repercussions.
   • **HOA Regulations:** If the property is governed by a homeowners association, adhere to their rules and regulations to avoid fines or legal action.

• **Fair Housing Laws:** Familiarize yourself with fair housing laws to ensure compliance and prevent discrimination in rental or sales practices.

6. **Professional Assistance:** Legal Counsel, Consult with experienced real estate attorneys to guide you through complex legal processes and provide expert advice.

• **Real Estate Agents:** Work with reputable real estate agents who understand local market dynamics and can facilitate smoother transactions.

• **Financial Advisors:** Seek advice from financial professionals to ensure your investment aligns with your long-term financial goals.

Common Mistakes to Avoid

1. **Skipping Due Diligence:** Failing to conduct thorough due diligence can lead to unforeseen issues post-transaction.

2. **Incomplete Documentation:** Incomplete or inaccurate documentation can result in legal disputes and delays.

3. **Ignoring Legal Advice:** Disregarding legal advice or attempting to navigate complex legal matters without professional assistance can be risky.

4. **Overlooking Regulations:** Ignoring zoning laws, building codes, or other regulations can result in costly penalties or inability to utilize the property as intended.

5. **Rushing Transactions:** Rushing into a transaction without careful consideration of all terms and implications can lead to regrettable decisions.

Navigating the pathways in law and documentation in real estate requires meticulous attention to detail, adherence to regulations, and reliance on professional expertise. By avoiding common mistakes and prioritizing thoroughness, you can mitigate risks and ensure successful property transactions.

Ignoring legal counsel and doing due diligence

Real estate transactions are intricate affairs that involve numerous legal intricacies and financial commitments. Ignoring the advice of legal counsel and neglecting due diligence can lead to significant and often costly mistakes. Here's a comprehensive exploration of the risks involved:

1. **Ignoring Legal Counsel:** Misinterpretation of Contracts, Legal documents in real estate transactions can be complex and laden with legal jargon. Without the guidance of legal counsel, individuals may misinterpret crucial terms or overlook important clauses, leaving them vulnerable to unfavorable terms or legal disputes.

- **Exposure to Legal Risks:** Real estate transactions involve a multitude of legal risks, including zoning violations, title defects, and contract breaches. Legal counsel can help identify and mitigate these risks, ensuring that the transaction proceeds smoothly and legally.
- **Lack of Negotiation Skills:** Legal professionals are adept at negotiating terms that are favorable to their clients. Without legal counsel, individuals may lack the negotiation skills necessary to secure advantageous terms in real estate transactions, potentially resulting in financial losses or missed opportunities.

2. **Neglecting Due Diligence:** Hidden Liabilities. Failure to conduct thorough due diligence can result in unforeseen liabilities, such as undisclosed property defects, outstanding liens, or environmental contamination. These hidden liabilities can lead to costly legal battles or financial losses down the line.

- **Inaccurate Valuation:** Due diligence plays a crucial role in accurately valuing a property. Without proper investigation, individuals may overpay for a property or underestimate its true value, leading to financial repercussions.

• **Regulatory Compliance Issues:** Neglecting due diligence can result in non-compliance with regulatory requirements, such as zoning laws, building codes, or environmental regulations. Violating these regulations can result in fines, penalties, or even the inability to use the property as intended.

Common Mistakes and Consequences

1. **Relying Solely on Seller Representations**: Believing everything the seller says without independent verification can lead to unpleasant surprises post-purchase.
2. **Skipping Title Search:** Failing to conduct a thorough title search can result in undiscovered liens or ownership disputes, clouding the buyer's ownership rights.
3. **Foregoing Property Inspection:** Skipping a property inspection can result in overlooking structural defects or safety hazards, exposing the buyer to potential safety risks or costly repairs.
4. **Disregarding Legal Advice:** Ignoring legal advice or attempting to navigate complex legal matters independently can result in costly legal battles or contractual disputes.
5. **Underestimating Financial Risks:** Neglecting financial due diligence can lead to overleveraging

or investing in properties with inadequate return potential, resulting in financial losses.

Ignoring legal counsel and neglecting due diligence in real estate transactions is a recipe for disaster. The risks include legal disputes, financial losses, and missed opportunities. By seeking expert legal advice and conducting thorough due diligence, individuals can mitigate these risks and ensure successful and legally sound real estate transactions.

Inaccurate or lacking documentation and breaking zoning laws and regulations

In the dynamic world of real estate, accurate documentation and adherence to zoning laws and regulations are paramount. Yet, many transactions encounter hurdles due to inaccuracies or oversights in documentation, as well as violations of zoning laws. Understanding the implications of these mistakes is crucial for all parties involved in real estate transactions.

The Importance of Accurate Documentation:

1. **Legal Standing:** Accurate documentation establishes the legal framework of property ownership, ensuring clarity and minimizing disputes.
2. **Financial Security:** Incorrect documentation can lead to financial losses through legal battles, fines, or invalidated transactions.
3. **Transaction Efficiency:** Clear and accurate documentation expedites transactions, reducing delays and associated costs.
4. **Trust and Reputation:** Maintaining accurate documentation builds trust among stakeholders and enhances the reputation of real estate professionals.

Common Documentation Mistakes:

1. **Incomplete Titles:** Missing or incomplete title documents can cloud ownership rights and hinder property transactions.
2. **Errors in Property Surveys:** Inaccurate surveys may result in boundary disputes or encroachments, complicating property transfers.

3. **Faulty Disclosures:** Failure to disclose pertinent information, such as property defects or legal issues, can lead to legal liabilities.

4. **Outdated Documentation**: Failure to update documents in line with changes in ownership or regulations can lead to complications during transactions.

Understanding Zoning Laws and Regulations:

1. **Purpose and Scope:** Zoning laws regulate land use and development, ensuring compatibility between properties and their surrounding environment.

2. **Compliance Requirements:** Zoning regulations dictate permissible land uses, building heights, setbacks, and other factors crucial for property development.

3. **Consequences of Violations:** Violating zoning laws can result in fines, legal injunctions, or even demolition orders, halting projects and causing financial losses.

4. **Due Diligence**: Conducting thorough due diligence on zoning regulations is essential to avoid costly violations and ensure compliance.

Common Zoning Violations:

1. **Unauthorized Land Use:** Operating a business or building structures inconsistent with zoning

regulations can lead to penalties and forced closures.

2. **Building Code Violations:** Failure to adhere to building codes or obtain necessary permits can result in fines and project delays.

3. **Setback Infringements:** Building structures too close to property lines or public rights-of-way can violate setback requirements, triggering legal action.

4. **Environmental Non-compliance:** Ignoring environmental regulations, such as wetland protection or hazardous materials disposal, can lead to severe penalties and reputational damage.

Mitigating Risks and Ensuring Compliance:

1. **Consultation with Experts**: Engage legal counsel, real estate agents, and land use professionals to navigate complex documentation and zoning requirements.

2. **Conduct Comprehensive Due Diligence:** Thoroughly review property documentation, conduct surveys, and verify zoning compliance before proceeding with transactions.

3. **Regular Updates and Reviews**: Stay informed about changes in regulations and update documentation accordingly to maintain compliance.

4. **Proactive Resolution of Issues**: Address any discrepancies or potential violations promptly to mitigate risks and maintain transaction integrity.

Inaccurate documentation and zoning violations pose significant risks in real estate transactions, potentially leading to financial losses, legal disputes, and reputational damage. By prioritizing accuracy, conducting thorough due diligence, and adhering to zoning regulations, stakeholders can mitigate these risks and ensure successful transactions. Collaboration with experts and proactive resolution of issues are essential for navigating the complexities of real estate transactions and safeguarding the interests of all parties involved.

Chapter 5. Ignoring Rental Market Dynamics

In the realm of real estate investing, understanding and adapting to rental market dynamics is paramount. Ignoring these fluctuations can lead to significant financial setbacks and missed opportunities for investors. This comprehensive content delves into the consequences of neglecting rental market dynamics and offers insights on how to navigate them effectively.

Understanding Rental Market Dynamics:
Rental market dynamics encompass various factors such as supply and demand, economic conditions, demographic trends, and local regulations. These elements influence rental prices, vacancy rates, and overall investment viability.

Consequences of Ignoring Rental Market Dynamics:

1. **Financial Losses**: Failing to assess rental market trends can result in overpaying for properties or setting unrealistic rental rates, leading to decreased profitability or even negative cash flow.

2. **Vacancy Issues:** Ignoring shifts in demand may result in prolonged vacancies, impacting cash flow and increasing carrying costs for investors.
3. **Inability to Compete:** Neglecting rental market dynamics can leave investors at a disadvantage compared to competitors who adapt their strategies based on current market conditions.
4. **Missed Opportunities:** Failure to recognize emerging trends or underserved niches in the rental market can result in missed opportunities for higher returns on investment.
5. **Regulatory Risks:** Ignoring local rental market regulations and compliance requirements can expose investors to legal and financial liabilities.

Strategies for Navigating Rental Market Dynamics:

1. **Market Research**: Conduct thorough research on local rental market trends, including vacancy rates, rental prices, demographic shifts, and economic indicators.
2. **Flexibility in Pricing:** Stay agile with rental pricing strategies to remain competitive and responsive to market fluctuations.
3. **Property Maintenance**: Ensure that properties are well-maintained and meet market expectations to attract and retain tenants.
4. **Diversification**: Spread investment across different properties or geographic locations to

mitigate risks associated with specific rental markets.

5. **Professional Guidance:** Seek advice from real estate professionals, property managers, and market analysts to make informed decisions.

Ignoring rental market dynamics in real estate investing is a costly mistake that can lead to financial losses, missed opportunities, and regulatory risks. By understanding and adapting to market fluctuations, investors can enhance their profitability and resilience in the ever-changing real estate landscape. With careful research, flexibility, and strategic planning, investors can navigate rental market dynamics effectively and capitalize on opportunities for long-term success.

Failing to Conduct Market Analysis

Once upon a time, there was an ambitious real estate developer named Alex. With dreams of building a luxurious condominium complex, Alex dove headfirst into the project without conducting thorough market analysis. Confident in their vision,

Alex ignored the warnings of seasoned investors and experts.

Excited by the prospect of creating a landmark property, construction began swiftly. The sleek designs and premium amenities seemed destined to attract affluent buyers. However, as the project neared completion, signs of trouble emerged.

The local economy had shifted, leaving potential buyers hesitant to invest in high-end properties. Additionally, a competitor had launched a similar project nearby, saturating the market and driving down demand.

Despite these warning signs, Alex pressed on, convinced that the allure of their development would prevail. But as the units hit the market, reality struck hard. The lack of demand led to sluggish sales and mounting pressure from creditors.

Desperate to salvage the situation, Alex slashed prices and offered generous incentives, but it was too little, too late. The project hemorrhaged money, and the once-promising venture turned into a financial nightmare.

In the end, Alex was forced to sell the property at a significant loss, tarnishing their reputation and leaving behind a cautionary tale of the importance of market analysis in real estate ventures. It was a costly lesson learned too late, serving as a reminder that success in real estate requires more than just vision—it demands careful research and strategic planning.

In the dynamic world of real estate, overlooking the importance of market analysis can lead to disastrous outcomes. Whether it's a residential development or a commercial project, failing to understand the nuances of the market can result in significant financial losses and missed opportunities.

Market analysis is crucial for several reasons:

1. **Understanding Demand:** Without a thorough understanding of market demand, developers risk building properties that fail to attract buyers or tenants. This can lead to prolonged vacancies and reduced profitability.

2. **Identifying Competition**: Ignoring the competitive landscape can leave developers blindsided by rival projects offering similar or better amenities at more competitive prices. This can erode demand for their own properties and undermine their viability.

3. **Assessing Pricing Strategies:** Pricing is a delicate balance in real estate. Without proper market analysis, developers may set prices too high, deterring potential buyers, or too low, leaving money on the table.

4. **Anticipating Trends:** Markets are constantly evolving, influenced by factors such as demographics, economic conditions, and consumer preferences. Failing to stay abreast of these trends

can result in investments that quickly become outdated or irrelevant.

5. **Mitigating Risks**: Market analysis helps identify potential risks and uncertainties, allowing developers to implement mitigation strategies and safeguard their investments against unforeseen challenges.

neglecting market analysis is a recipe for disaster in real estate. Developers must prioritize thorough research and analysis to ensure their projects are strategically positioned to capitalize on opportunities and mitigate risks in today's competitive market landscape.

Neglecting Market Trends and Analysis

Neglecting market trends and analysis in real estate can be a costly mistake for investors, buyers, and sellers alike. Failing to stay informed about the current state of the market can lead to missed opportunities, overpaying for properties, or selling below market value.

Understanding market trends allows investors to make informed decisions about when to buy, sell, or hold onto properties. Without this insight, they may find themselves investing in areas that are experiencing declining property values or oversaturated markets.

For buyers, neglecting market analysis can result in purchasing a property at an inflated price or in an area that doesn't hold its value over time. It's essential to assess factors such as local economic conditions, supply and demand dynamics, and upcoming developments that could impact property values.

Similarly, sellers who ignore market trends may struggle to attract buyers or receive lower offers than expected. By staying informed about market conditions, sellers can price their properties competitively and leverage market trends to their advantage.

In today's fast-paced real estate market, where conditions can change rapidly, staying ahead of the curve is crucial. Regularly monitoring market trends and conducting thorough analysis can help mitigate risks and maximize returns in real estate transactions.

Excessive Reduction in Property Value

In the dynamic world of real estate, property values can fluctuate due to various factors such as market trends, economic conditions, and property-specific attributes. While it's common for property owners to seek ways to enhance the value of their assets, there's a lesser-known pitfall that can occur – excessive reduction in property value.

Understanding Excessive Reduction in Property Value:

Excessive reduction in property value refers to the situation where property owners inadvertently diminish the value of their assets beyond what is necessary or reasonable. There are several reasons why this could occur, including

1. **Over-renovation**: While renovations can add value to a property, going overboard with high-end upgrades or making changes that don't align with the neighborhood's standard can lead to diminishing returns. Over-renovating can result in inflated costs that are not reflected in the property's market value, leading to a reduced return on investment.

2. **Neglecting Maintenance:** Failure to address maintenance issues in a timely manner can significantly detract from a property's value over time. Deferred maintenance can lead to deterioration of the property's condition, lowering its appeal to potential buyers and reducing its market value.

3. **Misguided Improvements:** Making improvements that do not align with the preferences or needs of potential buyers can result in a reduction in property value. For example, investing in features or amenities that are not in demand in the local market can fail to generate a return on investment and may even decrease the property's overall appeal.

4. **Environmental Factors**: External factors such as environmental pollution, proximity to hazardous sites, or natural disasters can negatively impact property values. Failure to consider these factors before purchasing or investing in a property can lead to unexpected declines in value over time.

Avoiding the Pitfall:

To avoid the trap of excessive reduction in property value, property owners should:
• Conduct thorough market research to understand the preferences and trends in the local real estate market.
• Consult with real estate professionals, such as appraisers and agents, to assess the potential

impact of proposed renovations or improvements on the property's value.
• Prioritize regular maintenance and address any issues promptly to preserve the property's condition and value.
• Consider the long-term implications of environmental factors on the property's value and factor them into investment decisions.

While enhancing the value of a property is a common goal for real estate investors and homeowners alike, it's essential to avoid the pitfall of excessive reduction in property value. By carefully considering market dynamics, making informed investment decisions, and prioritizing maintenance and upkeep, property owners can safeguard their investments and maximize their returns in the ever-evolving real estate landscape.

Chapter 6: Oversights of Management and Maintenance

Effective management and maintenance are crucial components in the real estate industry, ensuring properties retain their value and tenants remain satisfied. However, several oversights often plague these processes, leading to unnecessary expenses and tenant dissatisfaction.

1. **Neglecting Regular Inspections:** Failing to conduct routine inspections can result in unnoticed maintenance issues escalating into costly repairs. Regular inspections help identify issues early, allowing for prompt intervention and cost-effective solutions.

2. **Ignoring Tenant Feedback:** Disregarding tenant complaints or feedback can lead to dissatisfaction and increased tenant turnover. It's essential to actively listen to tenant concerns and address them promptly to maintain tenant satisfaction and retention.

3. **Deferred Maintenance:** Postponing necessary maintenance tasks to save costs can backfire in the

long run. Deferred maintenance not only decreases property value but also increases the likelihood of more significant issues arising over time, leading to higher repair expenses.

4.**Lack of Budget Planning:** Inadequate budget planning can hinder effective management and maintenance efforts. Failing to allocate sufficient funds for routine maintenance and unexpected repairs can lead to financial strain and compromised property conditions.

5.**Inadequate Training for Staff:** Insufficient training for property management and maintenance staff can result in subpar service delivery. Properly trained staff are better equipped to handle maintenance tasks efficiently and effectively, ultimately benefiting property owners and tenants alike.

6.**Failure to Embrace Technology:** Not leveraging technology tools for property management and maintenance can lead to inefficiencies and missed opportunities for optimization. Implementing software solutions for task management, reporting, and communication can streamline operations and enhance overall effectiveness.

7.**Ignoring Sustainability Practices:** Overlooking sustainability initiatives can lead to higher operating costs and environmental impact. Embracing energy-efficient upgrades, waste reduction strategies, and green building practices not only benefits the environment but also improves property value and appeal to tenants.

By addressing these common oversights, real estate professionals can enhance their management and maintenance practices, ultimately leading to improved property performance, tenant satisfaction, and long-term profitability.

The Costly Errors of Inadequate Property Management Techniques

In the world of real estate, success hinges not only on acquiring properties but also on effectively managing them. Unfortunately, inadequate property management techniques can lead to a cascade of costly mistakes that erode profits and tarnish reputations. From neglecting routine maintenance to poor tenant screening, here are some common pitfalls to avoid:

1.**Neglecting Routine Maintenance:** Overlooking regular upkeep can result in minor issues snowballing into major repairs. Ignoring tasks like HVAC servicing, plumbing checks, and roof inspections can lead to costly emergencies down the line.

2.**Ignoring Tenant Concerns:** Failing to address tenant complaints promptly can escalate issues and lead to dissatisfaction, higher turnover rates, and even legal disputes. Good communication and swift resolution of concerns are crucial for tenant retention and overall property satisfaction.

3.**Poor Tenant Screening:** Rushing through the tenant screening process or skipping essential background checks can result in problematic tenants who default on rent, damage property, or cause disturbances. Thorough screening, including credit checks, rental history verification, and references, is vital for securing reliable tenants.

4.**Inadequate Lease Agreements**: Using generic or outdated lease agreements without considering specific property needs or local regulations can leave property owners vulnerable to legal issues or disputes. Tailoring lease agreements to address property-specific requirements and legal obligations is essential for protecting both parties' interests.

5.**Lack of Financial Planning:** Failing to budget effectively for property expenses, including maintenance, taxes, insurance, and unexpected costs, can strain finances and disrupt cash flow. A comprehensive financial plan that accounts for all expenses and allows for contingencies is crucial for sustainable property management.

6.**Failure to Adapt to Market Trends**: Neglecting to stay informed about local market trends, rental demand, and competitive pricing can result in missed opportunities for maximizing rental income or optimizing property value. Continuously monitoring market dynamics and adjusting strategies accordingly is essential for staying competitive.

7.**Inadequate Risk Management**: Overlooking insurance coverage, liability protection, and emergency preparedness measures can leave property owners vulnerable to significant financial losses in the event of accidents, natural disasters, or legal claims. Implementing comprehensive risk management strategies is vital for safeguarding investments.

8.**Ineffective Communication with Stakeholders**: Poor communication with tenants, contractors, and other stakeholders can lead to misunderstandings, delays, and inefficiencies in property management processes. Establishing clear channels of communication and fostering positive relationships with all parties involved is essential for smooth operations.

effective property management requires diligence, foresight, and attention to detail. By avoiding the pitfalls of inadequate management techniques and implementing best practices, property owners can protect their investments, enhance property value, and cultivate positive tenant experiences.

Ignored Maintenance and Repair Problems

In the world of real estate management, overlooking maintenance and repair issues can lead to significant headaches down the road. From minor inconveniences to major structural damage, neglecting these problems can have costly consequences for property owners and managers. Here are some common mistakes associated with ignored maintenance and repair problems in real estate:

1. **Deferred Maintenance:** One of the most common mistakes is deferring necessary maintenance tasks. While it may seem like a cost-saving measure in the short term, ignoring maintenance issues can result in more extensive and expensive repairs later on. For example, failing to fix a leaky roof can lead to water damage and mold growth, requiring extensive remediation and repair work.

2. **Lack of Regular Inspections**: Without regular inspections, property managers may miss early signs of potential maintenance issues. Inspections allow managers to identify problems early on and address them before they escalate into more

significant issues. Ignoring routine inspections can lead to unnoticed issues, such as plumbing leaks, electrical problems, or structural defects.

3.**Failure to Prioritize Repairs**: When faced with multiple maintenance issues, some property owners or managers may prioritize cosmetic improvements over essential repairs. While aesthetic upgrades can enhance a property's appeal, neglecting critical repairs, such as fixing faulty wiring or repairing a foundation, can compromise the safety and integrity of the building.

4.**Ignoring Tenant Reports:** Tenants are often the first to notice maintenance problems within a property. Ignoring or dismissing tenant reports of issues such as plumbing leaks, heating or cooling problems, or pest infestations can lead to tenant dissatisfaction and turnover. Property managers should prioritize addressing tenant concerns promptly to maintain tenant satisfaction and retention.

5. **Failing to Plan for Maintenance Costs**: Many property owners fail to budget adequately for ongoing maintenance and repair expenses. Ignoring the need for a maintenance budget can result in financial strain when unexpected repairs arise. Setting aside funds for routine maintenance and creating a reserve for emergencies can help mitigate the financial impact of maintenance issues.

6.**Neglecting Safety Concerns**: Ignoring safety-related maintenance issues can expose property owners to liability risks. Whether it's failing to repair broken handrails, addressing fire code violations, or neglecting to maintain smoke detectors, overlooking safety concerns can lead to legal and financial consequences in the event of an accident or injury on the property.

7.**Not Seeking Professional Help**: Attempting to DIY maintenance and repairs or hiring unqualified individuals can exacerbate problems rather than solve them. Property owners and managers should enlist the expertise of qualified contractors and maintenance professionals to ensure that repairs are done correctly and to code.

ignoring maintenance and repair problems in real estate can have serious repercussions, including decreased property value, tenant dissatisfaction, and legal liabilities. Property owners and managers must prioritize proactive maintenance, regular inspections, and prompt repairs to safeguard their investments and ensure the safety and satisfaction of tenants. By avoiding these common mistakes, real estate professionals can maintain the long-term health and profitability of their properties.

Inability to Plan for Emergencies

The Pitfall of Inability to Plan for Emergencies in Real Estate: In the dynamic world of real estate investment, success often hinges on foresight and strategic planning. However, one common mistake that can lead to significant financial setbacks is the failure to adequately plan for emergencies. Whether it's unexpected repairs, market downturns, or natural disasters, being ill-prepared can quickly turn a promising investment into a financial burden.

Underestimating the Importance of Emergency Funds:

One of the primary errors investors make is underestimating the importance of having sufficient emergency funds. In real estate, emergencies can arise at any time, from sudden structural issues to legal disputes. Without a robust financial buffer, investors may find themselves scrambling to cover expenses, leading to cash flow problems and potential foreclosure.

Neglecting Property Inspections and Maintenance:

Another critical aspect of emergency preparedness is routine property inspections and maintenance. Neglecting these tasks can result in minor issues escalating into costly emergencies. For instance, a small leak left unchecked can lead to extensive water damage, impacting both the property's value and the investor's bottom line. By staying proactive and addressing maintenance issues promptly, investors can mitigate the risk of emergencies and preserve the property's long-term value.

Failure to Secure Adequate Insurance Coverage:

Insurance serves as a vital safeguard against unforeseen events in real estate investment. However, failing to secure adequate coverage can leave investors exposed to substantial financial liabilities. From property damage to liability claims, a comprehensive insurance policy can provide crucial protection and peace of mind. It's essential for investors to regularly review their insurance policies to ensure they adequately cover potential emergencies.

Ignoring Local Regulations and Zoning Laws:

Navigating local regulations and zoning laws is essential for real estate investors to avoid legal emergencies. Failure to comply with these regulations can result in fines, legal disputes, and even property seizures. Thorough due diligence and consultation with legal experts can help investors stay compliant and mitigate the risk of costly legal entanglements.

Overlooking Market Volatility and Economic Downturns:

Market volatility and economic downturns are inherent risks in real estate investment. Overlooking these factors and assuming perpetual market growth can leave investors vulnerable to financial crises. Conducting comprehensive market research and stress-testing investment strategies against various economic scenarios can help investors prepare for potential downturns and minimize their impact on investment portfolios.

the inability to plan for emergencies is a critical mistake that real estate investors must avoid at all costs. By prioritizing the establishment of emergency funds, proactive property maintenance, securing adequate insurance coverage, adhering to local regulations, and anticipating market fluctuations, investors can mitigate risks and safeguard their investments against unforeseen emergencies. Ultimately, prudent planning and preparedness are indispensable pillars of success in the dynamic landscape of real estate investment.

Chapter 7: Mistakes in Deal-Making and Negotiation

In the heart of the bustling city, where skyscrapers reached for the sky like giants, there stood a modest real estate firm run by a man named Marcus. Marcus was known for his shrewd negotiation tactics and his ability to strike lucrative deals. However, even the most seasoned professionals can stumble when blinded by ambition.

One sunny morning, Marcus received a call from a wealthy investor interested in purchasing a prime piece of commercial property. The offer was tempting, and Marcus saw dollar signs flashing before his eyes. Eager to close the deal and reap the rewards, he hastily agreed to the investor's terms without thoroughly examining the contract.

As the ink dried on the agreement, Marcus celebrated his apparent victory. However, his joy was short-lived when he discovered a critical error in the contract. Due to his oversight, he had agreed to a significantly lower selling price than what the property was worth. Panic gripped Marcus as he realized the magnitude of his mistake.

Desperate to salvage the situation, Marcus scrambled to rectify the error, but the investor refused to renegotiate. The deal was done, and Marcus was left to face the consequences of his carelessness. Word of his blunder spread quickly, tarnishing his reputation in the real estate community.

Determined to learn from his mistake, Marcus vowed to approach future negotiations with caution and diligence. He sought guidance from seasoned mentors, honed his negotiation skills, and triple-checked every contract before signing. Over time, Marcus regained the trust of his peers and rebuilt his reputation as a savvy deal-maker.

The tale of Marcus served as a cautionary reminder to all in the real estate industry: haste and greed can lead to costly mistakes. In the world of negotiation and deal-making, patience, thoroughness, and a keen eye for detail are the keys to success.

Mistakes in deal-making and negotiation can be costly in the real estate industry, impacting both parties involved. Here are few common mistakes to avoid.

1. **Lack of Preparation**: Failing to research market trends, property values, and comparable sales can weaken your negotiating position and lead to unfavorable deals.
2. **Overlooking Due Diligence**: Rushing through the due diligence process or neglecting to conduct thorough inspections can result in unexpected issues post-purchase, such as structural problems or legal encumbrances.
3. **Ignoring Emotional Factors**: Letting emotions dictate negotiations can cloud judgment and lead to impulsive decisions. It's crucial to stay objective and focused on the facts.
4. **Failing to Communicate Effectively**: Miscommunication or lack of clear communication can lead to misunderstandings, delays, and disputes. Clearly articulate your needs, concerns, and expectations throughout the negotiation process.
5. **Neglecting to Seek Professional Advice**: Attempting to navigate complex real estate transactions without seeking advice from experienced professionals, such as real estate agents, attorneys, or financial advisors, can increase the likelihood of making costly mistakes.

6. **Being Inflexible**: Stubbornness or rigidity in negotiations can hinder progress and prevent mutually beneficial agreements. Remain open to compromise and explore creative solutions to reach a satisfactory outcome for all parties involved.

By recognizing and avoiding these common mistakes, real estate professionals can enhance their negotiating skills and achieve more successful deals in the competitive real estate market.

Poor Ability to Negotiate

Negotiation is a essential skill in the real estate industry. Whether you're buying, selling, or leasing property, your ability to negotiate effectively can significantly impact the outcome of the transaction. Unfortunately, many people make mistakes that hinder their negotiating power, leading to unfavorable deals or missed opportunities. In this comprehensive guide, we'll explore some common pitfalls associated with poor negotiation skills in real estate and provide tips on how to avoid them.

1. **Lack of Preparation**: One of the biggest mistakes in real estate negotiation is failing to prepare adequately. Without a clear understanding

of your goals, priorities, and alternatives, you may find yourself at a disadvantage during negotiations. Before entering into any negotiation, take the time to research the market, understand current trends, and gather relevant information about the property in question. This preparation will empower you to make informed decisions and negotiate from a position of strength.

2. **Failure to Establish Clear Objectives**: Another common mistake is a lack of clarity regarding your objectives. Whether you're a buyer, seller, or agent, it's essential to define your goals and priorities before engaging in negotiations. Are you primarily focused on price, terms, or timing? What concessions are you willing to make, and which are non-negotiable? By establishing clear objectives upfront, you can avoid getting sidetracked during negotiations and increase your chances of achieving a favorable outcome.

3. **Ineffective Communication:** Effective communication is key to successful negotiation. Poor communication skills, such as talking too much, not listening actively, or failing to articulate your position clearly, can undermine your efforts and lead to misunderstandings. To improve your communication during negotiations, focus on active listening, ask clarifying questions, and express your needs and concerns assertively but respectfully. Remember that negotiation is a dialogue, not a monologue, and strive to find common ground with the other party.

4. **Fear of Confrontation:** Many people avoid confrontation during negotiations for fear of appearing aggressive or causing conflict. However, avoiding difficult conversations can actually be detrimental to the negotiation process. It's essential to address issues head-on and advocate for your interests assertively. Keep in mind that negotiation is not personal; it's about finding mutually beneficial solutions. By overcoming your fear of confrontation and advocating for yourself effectively, you can achieve better results in real estate negotiations.

5. **Ignoring Emotional Factors:** Real estate transactions can be emotional for all parties involved. Whether it's the excitement of buying a new home, the attachment to a property you're selling, or the stress of negotiating terms, emotions can cloud judgment and impede rational decision-making. It's crucial to recognize and manage your emotions during negotiations to avoid making impulsive or irrational decisions. Stay focused on your objectives, rely on facts and data, and take breaks if you need to regain perspective.

6. **Lack of Flexibility**: Negotiation is a dynamic process that often requires flexibility and creativity to reach a satisfactory agreement. Stubbornness or inflexibility can hinder progress and lead to impasse. While it's essential to advocate for your interests, it's also important to be open to compromise and explore alternative solutions. Consider the bigger picture and be willing to adjust your position if it serves your long-term goals.

Remember that a successful negotiation is one in which both parties feel satisfied with the outcome.

Effective negotiation skills are critical in the real estate industry, where deals are often complex and multifaceted. By avoiding common mistakes such as lack of preparation, failure to establish clear objectives, ineffective communication, fear of confrontation, ignoring emotional factors, and lack of flexibility, you can increase your chances of achieving favorable outcomes in real estate negotiations. Keep these tips in mind as you navigate the negotiation process, and don't hesitate to seek guidance from experienced professionals if needed.

Chapter 8: Mistakes in the Management and Selection of Tenants

Effective tenant management and selection are crucial for real estate investors and property managers to maintain a steady income stream and preserve property value. However, several common mistakes can lead to financial losses, legal issues, and property damage. In this comprehensive guide, we'll explore these mistakes and provide strategies to avoid them.

1. **Inadequate Screening Process:** One of the most critical mistakes in tenant selection is not conducting a thorough screening process. Rushing through or skipping background and credit checks can lead to tenants with poor payment history, criminal records, or previous evictions. This oversight can result in late payments, property damage, and legal complications down the line.

2. **Ignoring Red Flags**: Ignoring red flags during the screening process is another common mistake. Signs such as inconsistent rental history, gaps in employment, or reluctance to provide references

should not be overlooked. Failing to address these warning signs can lead to problematic tenants who may cause disturbances or fail to fulfill lease obligations.

3. **Lack of Clear Communication**: Poor communication between landlords or property managers and tenants can lead to misunderstandings and conflicts. Failure to establish clear guidelines regarding rent payment, maintenance requests, and property rules can result in disputes and tenant dissatisfaction. Regular communication and setting expectations from the outset are essential for a smooth landlord-tenant relationship.

4. **Neglecting Property Maintenance**: Neglecting property maintenance can lead to tenant dissatisfaction and turnover. Delaying repairs or failing to address maintenance issues promptly can create an unpleasant living environment and damage the property's reputation. Regular inspections and proactive maintenance can help prevent costly repairs and keep tenants satisfied.

5. **Inconsistent Enforcement of Lease Agreements:** Inconsistent enforcement of lease agreements can undermine the landlord's authority and lead to tenant disrespect for rules and regulations. Whether it's late rent payments, noise disturbances, or unauthorized alterations, landlords must consistently enforce lease terms to maintain order and uphold the integrity of the property.

6. **Failure to Conduct Regular Inspections**: Failure to conduct regular inspections is a mistake that can result in unnoticed property damage or lease violations. Periodic inspections allow landlords to identify maintenance issues early, ensure lease compliance, and address concerns before they escalate. Implementing a schedule for inspections can help landlords stay proactive in property management.

7. **Overlooking Legal Requirements**: Ignorance of local, state, and federal laws governing landlord-tenant relationships is a significant mistake that can lead to legal repercussions. From fair housing laws to eviction procedures, landlords must understand and comply with all legal requirements. Failure to do so can result in costly lawsuits, fines, and damage to the landlord's reputation.

8. **Failing to Adapt to Market Trends:** Failing to adapt to market trends and changing tenant preferences can lead to vacancies and decreased rental income. Landlords must stay informed about local rental market dynamics, including rental rates, tenant demographics, and amenities in demand. Being flexible and responsive to market trends can help landlords attract and retain quality tenants.

Effective tenant management and selection are essential for real estate investors and property managers to succeed in the rental market. By avoiding common mistakes such as inadequate screening, neglecting maintenance, and ignoring legal requirements, landlords can foster positive landlord-tenant relationships, mitigate risks, and maximize returns on their investments. Implementing proactive strategies and maintaining clear communication can help landlords create a thriving rental property business.

Chapter 9: Mistakes in Tax and Regulatory Compliance

Real estate investment can be lucrative, but navigating tax and regulatory compliance is crucial to avoid costly mistakes. Here are some common errors investors should be aware of:

1.**Misclassification of Expenses:** Failing to properly categorize expenses can lead to incorrect tax filings. Investors must distinguish between deductible operating expenses (such as repairs and maintenance) and capital expenses (such as improvements). Misclassifying expenses can result in overpaying taxes or triggering audits.

2.**Failure to Depreciate Assets:** Real estate investors can benefit from depreciation deductions, which allow them to recover the cost of income-producing properties over time. Not properly depreciating assets or using incorrect methods can result in missed tax savings. Investors should consult tax professionals to ensure accurate depreciation schedules.

3. **Ignoring Local Regulations**: Real estate investments are subject to various local regulations, including zoning laws, building codes, and landlord-tenant ordinances. Ignoring these regulations can result in fines, lawsuits, or even forced property closures. Investors should thoroughly research and comply with all applicable laws and regulations.

4. **Misreporting Rental Income**: Failure to report rental income accurately can lead to tax evasion charges and penalties. All rental income, including cash payments, must be reported to the IRS. Investors should maintain detailed records of rental income and expenses to support tax filings.

5. **Inadequate Record-Keeping**: Proper record-keeping is essential for tax compliance and audit defense. Investors should maintain organized records of all financial transactions, including property acquisitions, rental income, expenses, and depreciation. Digital accounting software can help streamline record-keeping processes.

6. **Failure to Plan for Capital Gains Taxes**: Selling real estate investments can trigger capital gains taxes, which vary based on factors such as holding period and tax bracket. Failing to plan for these taxes can erode investment returns. Investors should consider strategies such as 1031 exchanges or capital gains deferral to minimize tax liabilities.

7.**Not Utilizing Tax Credits and Incentives**: Many jurisdictions offer tax credits and incentives for real estate investments, such as historic rehabilitation credits or low-income housing tax credits. Failing to take advantage of these opportunities can result in missed tax savings. Investors should research available credits and incentives and incorporate them into their investment strategies.

8.**Overlooking State and Local Taxes**: In addition to federal taxes, real estate investors may be subject to state and local taxes, such as property taxes and transfer taxes. Ignoring these taxes can lead to unexpected liabilities and penalties. Investors should understand the tax obligations in each jurisdiction where they own property.

understanding and complying with tax and regulatory requirements are essential aspects of successful real estate investment. By avoiding common mistakes and seeking professional guidance when necessary, investors can maximize their returns and minimize their tax liabilities.

Lack of understanding of the benefits and implications of taxes

Real estate investment can be a lucrative endeavor, but it requires a comprehensive understanding of various financial factors, including taxes. Unfortunately, many individuals lack awareness of the benefits and implications of taxes in real estate investment, which can lead to missed opportunities and potential financial pitfalls.

Benefits of Understanding Taxes in Real Estate Investment:

1.**Tax Offsets**: Leveraging tax deductions is one of the main benefits of investing in real estate. Expenses such as mortgage interest, property taxes, maintenance costs, and depreciation can be deducted from taxable income, reducing the overall tax burden.

2.**Capital Gains Tax**: Profits earned from the sale of real estate assets are subject to capital gains tax. Understanding the tax implications of capital gains allows investors to strategize their investment decisions, such as timing property sales to optimize tax liabilities.

3.**1031 Exchange**: The IRS allows investors to defer capital gains taxes through a 1031 exchange, which involves reinvesting proceeds from the sale of one property into another similar property. This strategy enables investors to defer taxes and potentially increase their investment portfolio's value over time.

4.**Pass-Through Taxation**: Many real estate investments, such as partnerships and real estate investment trusts (REITs), offer pass-through taxation, where income generated from the investment is passed directly to the investors. Understanding this tax structure can provide investors with insights into their tax liabilities and overall investment returns.

Implications of Ignorance Towards Taxation:

1.**Higher Tax Liabilities**: Failing to capitalize on available tax deductions or overlooking tax planning strategies can result in higher tax liabilities for real estate investors, ultimately reducing their net returns.

2.**Missed Opportunities**: Without a thorough understanding of tax implications, investors may miss out on tax-efficient investment strategies, such as utilizing tax-deferred exchanges or structuring investments to maximize deductions.

3.**Legal Compliance Issues**: Ignorance of tax laws and regulations can lead to unintentional non-compliance, resulting in penalties, fines, and potential legal consequences for investors.

4.**Inefficient Portfolio Management**: A lack of understanding of tax implications can lead to inefficient portfolio management, where investors fail to optimize their investment strategies to minimize taxes and maximize returns over the long term.

a comprehensive understanding of taxes in real estate investment is essential for maximizing returns, minimizing tax liabilities, and ensuring legal compliance. Investors should educate themselves on relevant tax laws, leverage available tax deductions, and strategically plan their investments to achieve their financial goals effectively.

Failure to follow local regulations

Failing to adhere to local regulations in real estate investment can have serious consequences, both legally and financially. Local regulations govern various aspects of real estate development, ownership, and operation, including zoning laws, building codes, environmental regulations, and tax requirements. Ignoring or disregarding these regulations can result in:

1. **Legal Penalties**: Violating local regulations can lead to fines, lawsuits, or even criminal charges. Courts may order the demolition of non-compliant structures or impose hefty fines on property owners.
2. **Delays and Costs:** Non-compliance often leads to project delays and increased costs. Revising plans, obtaining permits retroactively, or settling legal disputes can significantly inflate expenses and prolong timelines.
3. **Reputation Damage**: Failing to follow local regulations can tarnish the reputation of real estate developers or investors. Negative publicity and community backlash may deter future investment opportunities and harm business relationships.
4. **Safety Risks**: Local regulations are designed to ensure the safety of occupants and the surrounding environment. Ignoring building codes or environmental protections can pose significant risks to public health and safety, leading to accidents, injuries, or environmental damage.
5. **Property Devaluation**: Non-compliant properties may face difficulties in resale or rental markets. Buyers and tenants often prefer properties that comply with regulations to avoid potential liabilities and uncertainties.

To mitigate the risks associated with non-compliance, real estate investors should:

• **Conduct thorough due diligence**: Research local regulations and consult with legal and regulatory experts to ensure compliance throughout the investment process.
• **Obtain necessary permits and approvals**: Secure permits, licenses, and approvals before initiating any construction or property development activities.
• **Engage with local stakeholders:** Build relationships with local authorities, community members, and advocacy groups to understand community concerns and align investment strategies with local development goals.
• **Regularly monitor regulatory changes:** Stay informed about evolving regulations and adapt investment strategies accordingly to maintain compliance.
• **Implement robust risk management practices**: Develop contingency plans and allocate resources to address potential regulatory challenges or unforeseen complications.

By prioritizing compliance with local regulations, real estate investors can mitigate legal, financial, and reputational risks while fostering sustainable and responsible development practices.

Chapter 10: Lack of Risk Management and Diversification

Real estate investment offers the allure of stable returns and tangible assets, but the failure to incorporate robust risk management and diversification strategies can lead to significant pitfalls. Here's a closer look at the dangers of overlooking these critical components:

1. **Vulnerability to Market Fluctuations**: Without diversification, a real estate portfolio becomes overly reliant on the performance of a single asset or market segment. Economic downturns, changes in interest rates, or shifts in consumer preferences can drastically impact property values, leading to substantial losses.

2. **Concentration Risk**: Investing solely in one type of property (e.g., residential, commercial, or industrial) or in a specific geographic location exposes investors to concentration risk. Localized economic downturns, regulatory changes, or demographic shifts can erode property values,

leaving investors with limited options for mitigating losses.

3. **Illiquidity**: Real estate investments are inherently illiquid, meaning they cannot be easily converted into cash. In the absence of a diversified portfolio, investors may struggle to sell properties quickly during times of financial distress, potentially leading to liquidity problems and forced sales at unfavorable prices.

4. **Lack of Portfolio Protection**: Risk management strategies such as insurance coverage, contingency funds, and hedging instruments provide essential safeguards against unforeseen events such as natural disasters, tenant defaults, or legal disputes. Failing to implement these measures leaves investors exposed to significant financial liabilities and operational disruptions.

5. **Missed Opportunities:** Diversification not only helps mitigate risk but also enables investors to capitalize on a broader range of investment opportunities. By allocating capital across different property types, geographic regions, and investment strategies, investors can optimize their risk-return profiles and enhance overall portfolio performance.

6. **Inadequate Due Diligence**: Effective risk management involves thorough due diligence to assess the quality and viability of potential investments. Neglecting this process increases the likelihood of investing in properties with hidden defects, regulatory issues, or unsustainable

revenue streams, ultimately undermining long-term profitability.

7. **Limited Flexibility**: A lack of diversification restricts investors' ability to adapt to changing market conditions or capitalize on emerging trends. By maintaining a diversified portfolio, investors can pivot their strategies, reallocate resources, and capitalize on new opportunities as they arise, thereby enhancing resilience and long-term growth prospects.

The absence of robust risk management and diversification strategies exposes real estate investors to a myriad of risks and limits their ability to optimize returns and navigate market uncertainties effectively. By prioritizing these essential components, investors can mitigate downside risks, enhance portfolio resilience, and position themselves for sustainable long-term success in the dynamic real estate market.

Concentration of Risk in One Asset or Location

Real estate investment offers lucrative opportunities for wealth accumulation and portfolio diversification. However, investors must be mindful of the inherent risks associated with concentrating their investments in a single asset or location. Concentration of risk in real estate investment refers to the situation where an investor's portfolio is heavily reliant on a specific property or geographic area, leaving them vulnerable to various economic, market, and environmental factors.

Factors Contributing to Concentration of Risk:

1. **Asset Dependency:** Investing all resources into a single property exposes investors to the specific risks associated with that asset. Any adverse events such as property damage, market depreciation, or vacancy can significantly impact the investment's value and potential returns.
2. **Geographic Concentration:** Focusing investments in a particular location can amplify risks associated with local economic conditions, regulatory changes, natural disasters, and demographic shifts. For instance, an area heavily reliant on a single industry may experience downturns if that industry faces challenges.

Key Risks of Concentration:

1. **Market Volatility:** Property values can fluctuate due to changing market conditions, affecting the overall profitability of the investment. In a concentrated portfolio, the impact of market volatility is magnified, potentially leading to substantial losses.
2. **Liquidity Challenges**: Selling a single property in a concentrated portfolio may be challenging, especially during market downturns or when the property is in an undesirable location. This lack of liquidity can hinder investors' ability to quickly reallocate resources or mitigate losses.
3. **Diversification Limitations**: Concentrated investments limit diversification opportunities, depriving investors of the benefits of spreading risk across different asset classes and geographic regions. Diversification is essential for reducing overall portfolio risk and enhancing long-term stability.

Strategies to Mitigate Concentration Risk:

1. **Portfolio Diversification:** Allocating investments across multiple properties, asset classes, and geographic regions can help mitigate concentration risk. Diversification spreads risk and reduces vulnerability to adverse events affecting a single asset or location.
2. **Thorough Due Diligence**: Conducting comprehensive due diligence before investing in any property is crucial. Evaluating market

fundamentals, property condition, rental demand, and potential risks can help investors make informed decisions and avoid overly risky investments.

3. **Risk Management Strategies**: Implementing risk management strategies such as insurance coverage, contingency planning, and regular property inspections can help mitigate the impact of unforeseen events on investment performance.

While real estate investment offers the potential for attractive returns, concentration of risk in a single asset or location can expose investors to significant vulnerabilities. By diversifying their portfolios, conducting thorough due diligence, and implementing effective risk management strategies, investors can minimize concentration risk and build more resilient investment portfolios capable of withstanding various market conditions.

Lack of Risk Mitigation Techniques

Real estate investment can be lucrative, but it also carries inherent risks. One significant challenge investors face is the lack of robust risk mitigation techniques. This is a thorough synopsis of the problem:

1. **Market Volatility**: Real estate markets can be highly volatile, subject to fluctuations influenced by economic conditions, government policies, and geopolitical events. Without proper risk mitigation strategies, investors may face significant losses during market downturns.

2. **Lack of Diversification**: Overconcentration in a particular type of property or geographic location can increase investment risk. Without diversification, investors are more

vulnerable to adverse events specific to a particular market segment or region.

3. **Financial Risk**: Real estate investments often require substantial capital, whether through purchasing properties outright or financing through loans. Failure to adequately manage financial risk, such as overleveraging or insufficient cash reserves, can lead to financial distress and potential foreclosure.

4. **Operational Risks**: Managing real estate properties involves various operational risks, including maintenance, tenant turnover, and regulatory compliance. Inadequate property management practices can

result in decreased property value, rental income loss, and legal liabilities.

5. **Market Timing**: Timing the market accurately is challenging, and mistimed investments can lead to missed opportunities or losses. Lack of effective timing strategies increases vulnerability to economic cycles and market fluctuations.

6. **Interest Rate Risk**: Real estate investments are sensitive to changes in interest rates, impacting borrowing costs and property valuations. Failure to anticipate and mitigate interest rate risk can affect investment returns and affordability.

7. **Environmental and Regulatory Risks**: Environmental hazards, zoning

regulations, and compliance requirements pose additional risks to real estate investments. Failure to conduct thorough due diligence on environmental factors and regulatory compliance can lead to unexpected costs and legal liabilities.

8. **Emerging Risks**: Rapid technological advancements, demographic shifts, and unforeseen events such as natural disasters or pandemics introduce new risks to the real estate sector. Lack of preparedness to address emerging risks can catch investors off guard and disrupt investment performance.

To mitigate these risks effectively, real estate investors should employ a comprehensive risk management strategy that includes diversification, thorough due diligence, financial analysis, contingency planning, and proactive monitoring of market trends and regulatory changes. Additionally, seeking guidance from experienced professionals, such as real estate agents, financial advisors, and legal experts, can help investors navigate complex risk factors and make informed investment decisions.

Chapter 11: Professional and Ethical Conduct Slips

In the realm of real estate investment, maintaining professional and ethical conduct is paramount for success and reputation. Professionalism and ethics serve as guiding principles that not only protect investors but also ensure fair dealings and positive outcomes for all parties involved. Here's a comprehensive overview of the significance of professional and ethical conduct slips in real estate investment:

1. **Transparency and Honesty**: Investors must adhere to the highest standards of transparency and honesty when dealing with clients, partners, and stakeholders. Providing accurate information about properties, market conditions, and investment risks is essential to building trust and credibility.

2. **Compliance with Laws and Regulations**: Real estate investors are subject to various laws and regulations at the local, state, and federal levels. Adhering to these legal requirements is not only a

matter of compliance but also a reflection of ethical responsibility. Violating laws or engaging in unethical practices can lead to legal consequences and damage to one's reputation.

3. **Confidentiality**: Respecting the confidentiality of sensitive information shared by clients or other parties is crucial in maintaining trust and professionalism. Investors must safeguard confidential data and refrain from disclosing it without proper authorization.

4. **Conflict of Interest Management**: Real estate investors often encounter situations where their personal interests may conflict with the interests of their clients or partners. Managing these conflicts ethically involves disclosing any potential conflicts upfront and taking measures to mitigate them fairly and transparently.

5. **Fair Treatment of All Parties:** Treating all parties involved in a real estate transaction with fairness and respect is fundamental to ethical conduct. This includes buyers, sellers, tenants, landlords, and other stakeholders. Discrimination or favoritism based on factors such as race, gender, religion, or socioeconomic status is unacceptable.

6. **Fiduciary Responsibility:** Investors who act as fiduciaries have a legal and ethical duty to prioritize their clients' interests above their own. This includes providing unbiased advice, acting in good faith, and avoiding conflicts of interest. Breaching fiduciary duties can result in legal liabilities and reputational damage.

7. **Professional Development and Education**: Staying informed about industry trends, best practices, and ethical standards is essential for real estate investors. Investing in continuous professional development and education helps individuals uphold ethical conduct and adapt to evolving market conditions.

8. **Accountability and Integrity:** Taking responsibility for one's actions and decisions demonstrates integrity and professionalism. Real estate investors should hold themselves accountable for upholding ethical standards, addressing mistakes or shortcomings, and maintaining transparency in their dealings.

9. **Community Engagement and Social Responsibility:** Real estate investors have a role to play in contributing positively to the communities where they operate. Engaging in philanthropic activities, supporting sustainable development initiatives, and adhering to environmental regulations are integral aspects of ethical conduct in real estate investment.

professional and ethical conduct slips serve as guiding principles for real estate investors to uphold integrity, transparency, and fairness in their dealings. By adhering to these standards, investors not only protect their own interests but also contribute to a more trustworthy and sustainable real estate industry.

Fiduciary duty breaches

Understanding Fiduciary Duty Breaches in Real Estate Investments.In the realm of real estate investment, fiduciary duty plays a pivotal role in safeguarding the interests of investors. A fiduciary is entrusted with the responsibility to act in the best interest of their clients, putting their needs above their own. When this duty is breached, it can have significant legal and financial consequences. Here's a comprehensive overview:

1. **Definition of Fiduciary Duty**:
   • Fiduciary duty is a legal obligation that requires individuals or entities, such as real estate agents, brokers, property managers, and investment advisors, to act in the best interest of their clients.
   • This duty encompasses aspects such as loyalty, confidentiality, full disclosure, and the duty to avoid conflicts of interest.

2. **Types of Fiduciary Duties**:

   • **Duty of Loyalty:** Requires the fiduciary to prioritize the client's interests over their own and to avoid any actions that could lead to a conflict of interest.
   • **Duty of Care**: Mandates that the fiduciary performs their duties with the level of care, skill,

and diligence that a prudent person would exercise in similar circumstances.
- **Duty of Disclosure**: Obliges the fiduciary to provide all relevant information to the client, ensuring transparency in all transactions.
- **Duty of Confidentiality**: Requires the fiduciary to keep all client information confidential, unless authorized to disclose it

3. **Breaches of Fiduciary Duty in Real Estate Investments:**

- **Self-Dealing**: When a fiduciary engages in transactions that benefit themselves at the expense of the client, such as purchasing property for personal gain without disclosing it to the client.
- **Conflict of Interest:** Occurs when the fiduciary's personal interests or relationships interfere with their ability to act in the client's best interest, leading to biased decision-making.
- **Misrepresentation**: Providing false or misleading information to the client regarding the property, its value, potential returns, or risks associated with the investment.
- **Negligence**: Failing to exercise due diligence in the management of the property or investment, resulting in financial loss for the client.

4. **Consequences of Breaching Fiduciary Duty**:

- **Legal Liability:** Fiduciaries who breach their duty may face lawsuits from clients seeking damages for financial losses incurred due to the breach.
- **Financial Penalties:** Courts may order fiduciaries to compensate clients for any losses suffered as a result of the breach, including punitive damages in cases of egregious misconduct.
- **Reputation Damage:** Breaches of fiduciary duty can tarnish the reputation of the fiduciary and their business, leading to loss of trust and credibility in the industry.

5. **Preventative Measures:**

- **Clear Communication**: Establish clear expectations and communication channels between fiduciaries and clients to ensure transparency and mutual understanding.
- **Written Agreements**: Document the terms of the fiduciary relationship in written agreements, outlining the duties and responsibilities of each party.
- **Continuing Education**: Fiduciaries should stay informed about relevant laws, regulations, and best practices in real estate investment to mitigate the risk of breaches.
- **Regular Monitoring:** Implement systems for monitoring and oversight to detect and address any potential conflicts of interest or breaches of duty promptly.

fiduciary duty breaches in real estate investments can have serious repercussions for both investors and fiduciaries. It's essential for fiduciaries to uphold their duty with integrity and diligence to maintain trust and protect the interests of their clients.

Conflict of interest concernsb

In the realm of real estate investment, conflict of interest concerns can arise due to various factors, potentially impacting the integrity and fairness of transactions. Here's a look at these concerns:

1. **Dual Agency**: When a real estate agent or broker represents both the buyer and seller in a transaction, conflicts of interest may arise. The agent may prioritize their commission over the best interests of either party, leading to biased advice or decisions.

2. **Undisclosed Relationships**: Investors should be wary of undisclosed relationships between parties involved in a transaction, such as a real estate agent having a personal relationship with a seller or buyer. These relationships can influence

negotiations and potentially disadvantage one party.

3. **Self-Dealing**: Real estate professionals, including property managers or developers, may engage in self-dealing by prioritizing their personal interests over those of their clients or investors. This could involve purchasing properties for their own benefit before presenting them to clients or diverting resources for personal gain.

4. **Insider Trading:** In the context of real estate investment trusts (REITs) or development projects, insider trading can occur when individuals with privileged information about a property or market exploit that information for personal gain. This can distort market dynamics and harm other investors.

5. **Kickbacks and Referral Fees:** Conflict of interest concerns can arise when real estate professionals receive kickbacks or referral fees for recommending specific properties, lenders, or service providers to their clients. This may lead to biased advice and decisions that are not in the best interest of the investor.

6. **Misrepresentation of Property**: Sellers, agents, or developers may misrepresent the characteristics or condition of a property to inflate its value or conceal defects. This can lead to investors making decisions based on false information, resulting in financial losses and legal repercussions.

7. **Fiduciary Duties:** Real estate professionals owe fiduciary duties to their clients, including the duty of loyalty and the duty to disclose material

information. Failure to fulfill these duties can lead to conflicts of interest and breaches of trust, potentially resulting in legal action.

To mitigate conflict of interest concerns in real estate investment, investors should conduct thorough due diligence, seek independent advice, and carefully review contracts and disclosures. Additionally, regulatory bodies and professional associations enforce ethical standards and guidelines to promote transparency and integrity in the industry.

Chapter 12: Results and Suggestions

Results:
Real estate investment yields a diverse range of results, influenced by various factors such as location, market conditions, property type, and investment strategy. Here are some key outcomes commonly observed in real estate investment:

1. **Capital Appreciation**: One of the primary benefits of real estate investment is the potential for property value appreciation over time. This occurs as demand for properties in desirable locations increases, leading to higher prices and capital gains for investors.
2. **Rental Income:** Investors can generate consistent cash flow through rental income by leasing out properties to tenants. This income stream can provide a steady source of revenue, helping to cover mortgage payments, maintenance costs, and generate profits.
3. **Tax Advantages**: Real estate investors can benefit from various tax incentives, including deductions for mortgage interest, property taxes, depreciation, and expenses related to property management. These tax advantages can help

minimize the overall tax burden and increase the profitability of investments.

4. **Portfolio Diversification**: Investing in real estate can diversify an investment portfolio, reducing overall risk exposure. Real estate often behaves differently from stocks, bonds, and other asset classes, providing a hedge against market volatility and economic downturns.

5. **Inflation Hedge:** Real estate is considered an effective hedge against inflation since property values and rental income tend to rise in tandem with inflationary pressures. As the cost of living increases, real estate investments can preserve wealth and purchasing power over time.

Suggestions:

While real estate investment offers numerous opportunities for wealth accumulation, it also presents certain risks and challenges. Here are some suggestions for maximizing returns and mitigating risks in real estate investment:

1. **Market Research**: Conduct thorough market research to identify emerging trends, demand-supply dynamics, and investment opportunities in target locations. Analyze factors such as population growth, job market stability, infrastructure development, and economic indicators to make informed investment decisions.

2. **Financial Analysis:** Perform detailed financial analysis, including cash flow projections, return on

investment (ROI) calculations, and sensitivity analysis to assess the feasibility and profitability of potential investments. Consider factors such as acquisition costs, financing options, operating expenses, and exit strategies to evaluate risk-adjusted returns.

3. **Risk Management:** Implement risk management strategies to mitigate potential risks associated with real estate investment, such as market volatility, tenant defaults, property damage, and regulatory changes. Diversify investments across different asset classes, geographic locations, and property types to spread risk and optimize portfolio performance.

4. **Due Diligence:** Conduct comprehensive due diligence before acquiring a property, including property inspections, title searches, environmental assessments, and legal reviews. Evaluate the condition of the property, its marketability, and any potential liabilities or encumbrances that may affect the investment's profitability.

5. **Professional Guidance**: Seek guidance from experienced real estate professionals, including real estate agents, property managers, appraisers, and attorneys, to navigate complex transactions and legal matters. Leverage their expertise and industry knowledge to identify opportunities, negotiate favorable terms, and mitigate risks throughout the investment process.

By implementing these suggestions and leveraging the potential results of real estate investment, investors can optimize their returns, build wealth, and achieve their financial goals over the long term.

The Value of Learning from Mistakes

Real estate investment, like any other venture, comes with its share of risks and challenges. However, it's often the mistakes made along the way that provide invaluable lessons for investors. Understanding and learning from these mistakes can significantly enhance one's success and longevity in the real estate market. Here are some key reasons why learning from mistakes is crucial in real estate investment:

1. **Identifying Weaknesses:** Mistakes highlight areas where an investor may have weaknesses, whether it's in due diligence, financial analysis, negotiation skills, or market understanding. Recognizing these weaknesses allows investors to focus on improving and strengthening their strategies.
2. **Refining Decision-Making Skills**: Making mistakes provides an opportunity to analyze

decisions and understand what went wrong. This process helps investors refine their decision-making skills, enabling them to make more informed and effective choices in the future.

3. **Avoiding Costly Errors:** Learning from mistakes can help investors avoid repeating costly errors. Whether it's overleveraging, underestimating renovation costs, or misjudging market trends, understanding past mistakes can prevent similar missteps in future investments.

4. **Building Resilience**: Real estate investment is not immune to setbacks and failures. Learning from mistakes fosters resilience and adaptability, essential qualities for navigating the ups and downs of the market. It teaches investors to bounce back stronger and more determined after facing challenges.

5. **Enhancing Risk Management**: Analyzing past mistakes allows investors to improve their risk management strategies. By understanding what led to a particular failure, investors can implement measures to mitigate similar risks in future investments, thereby safeguarding their capital and maximizing returns.

6. **Gaining Experience**: Every mistake is an opportunity to gain valuable experience. Over time, investors accumulate a wealth of knowledge that enhances their expertise in real estate investment. This experience becomes an invaluable asset in identifying opportunities and making sound investment decisions.

7. **Fostering Continuous Improvement**: Learning from mistakes is a continuous process that fosters personal and professional growth. Successful investors embrace failures as opportunities for improvement, constantly seeking to refine their skills and strategies to stay ahead in the competitive real estate market.

The value of learning from mistakes in real estate investment cannot be overstated. It provides investors with invaluable lessons, helps them identify weaknesses, refine decision-making skills, avoid costly errors, build resilience, enhance risk management, gain experience, and foster continuous improvement. By embracing failures and leveraging them as opportunities for growth, investors can increase their chances of long-term success in the dynamic world of real estate investment.

Techniques for Steering Clear of Typical Pitfalls

Real estate investment can be a lucrative venture, but it's not without its challenges. Avoiding common pitfalls is crucial for success in this competitive market. By employing the right techniques and strategies, investors can mitigate risks and maximize returns. Below are some key tactics for steering clear of typical pitfalls in real estate investment.

1. **Thorough Research and Due Diligence:**
   • Conduct comprehensive research on the local market, including property values, rental rates, vacancy rates, and economic trends.
   • Perform due diligence on prospective properties, inspecting them thoroughly for any issues or potential liabilities.
   • Verify the property's title, zoning regulations, and any pending legal or environmental issues that could affect its value.

2. **Financial Planning and Risk Management**:
   • Develop a detailed financial plan that includes budgeting for acquisition costs, ongoing expenses, and potential renovations or repairs.
   • Assess the risks associated with the investment, including market volatility, interest rate fluctuations, and unforeseen expenses.
   • Consider diversifying your real estate portfolio to spread risk across different types of properties and locations.

3. **Professional Guidance and Networking:**

• Seek advice from experienced real estate professionals, such as real estate agents, brokers, and property managers.

• Build a network of industry contacts, including fellow investors, contractors, and legal experts, who can provide valuable insights and support.

• Consider joining real estate investment groups or attending networking events to stay informed about market trends and opportunities.

4. **Conservative Financing and Cash Flow Management:**

• Avoid overleveraging by securing financing with favorable terms and reasonable interest rates.

• Calculate the property's potential cash flow accurately, taking into account all expenses and potential vacancies.

• Maintain adequate reserves for unexpected expenses, such as repairs, vacancies, or economic downturns.

5. **Long-Term Strategy and Exit Planning:**

• Develop a clear investment strategy with defined goals and timelines for achieving them.

• Consider the property's long-term appreciation potential and its ability to generate passive income over time.

• Have a contingency plan in place for exiting the investment, whether through sale, refinancing, or other means, if market conditions change.

Successful real estate investment requires careful planning, diligent research, and prudent decision-making. By employing these techniques and strategies, investors can navigate the complexities of the market and avoid common pitfalls. With patience, perseverance, and a strategic approach, real estate investment can be a rewarding and profitable endeavor.

Ongoing Learning and Development in real estate practice

Ongoing learning and development are crucial components of success in real estate practice, particularly in the realm of real estate investment. In an ever-evolving market, staying abreast of industry trends, regulations, and best practices is essential for professionals to thrive. Here's a comprehensive overview of ongoing learning and development in real estate investment:

1. **Market Analysis and Trends:** Continuous education enables real estate investors to conduct thorough market analyses, identifying emerging trends, and anticipating shifts in demand. This knowledge allows them to make informed decisions regarding property acquisitions, developments, and sales.

2. **Financial Analysis and Investment Strategies**: Ongoing learning equips investors with the skills to perform complex financial analyses, including cash flow projections, return on investment calculations, and risk assessments. This enables them to devise effective investment strategies tailored to their financial objectives and risk tolerance.

3. **Legal and Regulatory Compliance**: The regulatory landscape in real estate is dynamic, with laws and regulations frequently changing at local, state, and federal levels. Continuous education ensures investors stay compliant with relevant laws, such as zoning regulations, landlord-tenant laws, and tax codes, minimizing the risk of legal disputes and financial penalties.

4. **Property Management Practices**: For investors who own and manage rental properties, ongoing learning encompasses effective property management practices. This includes tenant screening, lease negotiation, maintenance and repairs, and conflict resolution techniques. By enhancing property management skills, investors can maximize rental income and maintain high occupancy rates.

5. **Technology Integration:** Advancements in technology have revolutionized the real estate industry, offering innovative tools and platforms to streamline processes and enhance decision-making. Ongoing learning enables investors to leverage these technologies effectively, whether it's using data analytics for market research or adopting property management software for efficient operations.

6. **Networking and Collaboration:** Learning doesn't just occur in formal educational settings; it also happens through networking and collaboration with industry peers. Engaging in professional associations, attending conferences, and participating in forums facilitate knowledge exchange, idea generation, and partnership opportunities, enriching investors' learning experiences.

7. **Adaptation to Economic Cycles:** Real estate markets are subject to economic cycles, including periods of growth, stability, and downturns. Continuous education equips investors with the skills to adapt their strategies accordingly, whether it involves capitalizing on opportunities during periods of growth or implementing risk mitigation measures during economic downturns.

Ongoing learning and development are integral to success in real estate investment. By continuously expanding their knowledge base, honing their skills, and staying attuned to industry developments, investors can navigate the complexities of the real estate market with confidence and achieve their financial goals.

Chapter 13: Unlocking success in real estate investment

Unlocking Success in Real Estate Investment," where we delve into the intricacies of navigating the dynamic world of real estate. Whether you're a seasoned investor or just dipping your toes into the market, this ebook will equip you with the knowledge and strategies needed to thrive in this lucrative industry.

1 **Understanding the Market**
• Explore different types of real estate investments: residential, commercial, industrial, and land.

- Analyze market trends, demographics, and economic indicators to identify lucrative opportunities.
- Learn about the importance of location, property appreciation, and rental income potential.

2 Setting Clear Goals
- Define your investment objectives, whether it's generating passive income, building wealth, or diversifying your portfolio.
- Establish short-term and long-term goals, and create a roadmap to achieve them.
- Determine your risk tolerance and investment timeframe.

3 Financial Planning and Budgeting
- Assess your financial situation, including your savings, income, debts, and credit score.
- Develop a realistic budget that accounts for acquisition costs, maintenance expenses, taxes, and contingencies.
- Explore financing options such as mortgages, loans, partnerships, or crowdfunding.

4 Property Selection and Due Diligence
- Conduct thorough research on potential properties, considering factors like location, condition, market demand, and zoning regulations.
- Perform comprehensive due diligence, including property inspections, title searches, and financial analysis.

- Evaluate the potential return on investment (ROI) and assess risks before making a purchase decision.

5 **Building a Professional Network**
- Cultivate relationships with real estate agents, brokers, attorneys, lenders, contractors, and property managers.
- Leverage their expertise, insights, and connections to streamline the investment process and mitigate risks.
- Join industry associations, attend networking events, and participate in online forums to expand your network and stay updated on industry trends.

6 **Implementing Effective Investment Strategies**
- Explore different investment strategies such as fix-and-flip, buy-and-hold, wholesaling, or real estate investment trusts (REITs).
- Diversify your portfolio across different property types, locations, and investment vehicles to minimize risk and maximize returns.
- Continuously monitor market conditions, adjust your strategies accordingly, and stay flexible in response to changing circumstances.

7 **Managing Properties and Maximizing Returns**
- Develop a proactive property management plan to maintain and enhance the value of your investments.

• Screen tenants rigorously, enforce lease agreements, and address maintenance issues promptly to minimize vacancies and maximize cash flow.
• Explore strategies to increase rental income, such as renovations, upgrades, or implementing amenities.

Congratulations on completing "Unlocking Success in Real Estate Investment." Armed with the knowledge and strategies outlined in this ebook, you're well-equipped to navigate the complexities of real estate investing and achieve your financial goals. Remember, success in real estate requires diligence, patience, and a willingness to continuously learn and adapt. Here's to your prosperous journey in the world of real estate investment!

Conclusion

avoiding common mistakes in real estate investment is essential for maximizing returns and minimizing risks. By recognizing and addressing pitfalls such as inadequate research, overleveraging, neglecting property management, and failing to adapt to market conditions, investors can enhance their chances of success in the dynamic world of real estate. Through prudent decision-making, continuous learning, and disciplined execution, investors can build sustainable and profitable real estate portfolios over time.

Prayers
"May we learn from our mistakes and grow wiser in our real estate investments. Grant us the courage to navigate challenges and the humility to seek guidance when needed and to succeed. Amen."

If you enjoyed the book, please consider leaving a review! Your feedback helps others discover it and also encourage me to write more. Thank you for reading and sharing your thoughts!

www.ingramcontent.com/pod-product-compliance
Lightning Source LLC
Chambersburg PA
CBHW050305230526
45471CB00005B/2038